CW01072491

THE FIRST YEAR

Coping with Widowhood

Vennie Anderson

outskirts press

Outskirts Press, Inc.
http://www.outskirtspress.com

Paperback ISBN: 978-1-9772-4456-7
Hardback ISBN: 978-1-9772-4477-2

To my longtime friend and fellow nurse, Doris Frey.
You were part of our journey from the first date
all the way to the end. Thank you for being there.

ACKNOWLEDGEMENTS

I'd like to thank Outskirts Press for doing an excellent job in breathing life into this book. As self-publishers, they were paid for their services; nevertheless, they did an outstanding job and deserve credit where credit is due.

I'd also like to proffer additional thanks to Elaine Simpson, my Outskirts Press author's representative, who shepherded me through the entire publishing process. She patiently listened to my lamentations and apologies for my lack of computer expertise and reassured me I was doing a good job of holding up my end of the publishing tasks.

Finally, I'd like to point out that I chose not to have the editors at Outskirts Press do any editing whatsoever to the journal entry portions of the book. Any errors therein are mine and not those of Outskirts Press.

Vennie Anderson, July 2021

TABLE OF CONTENTS

FOREWORD

"This isn't how it was supposed to be, you know," my fifty-four-year-old husband said to the young nurse starting an IV prior to his first—and what was to be the only—dose of chemotherapy. "We were supposed to grow old together," he went on. "Then she'd go first, and I'd be a dirty old man, chasing all the girls."

We were in Barnes Hospital in St. Louis, Missouri. I was sitting in a chair on the other side of the bed, and I could see that for a moment, the nurse was taken aback, until she saw the twinkle in his eyes.

She looked at me and said, "He's cute, isn't he?"

"He thinks he is," I replied dryly.

The evening before, in preparation for the chemotherapy, Wendell had been given a massive dose of a corticosteroid, which among other effects can result in mood elevation. Overnight he went from devastatingly ill to sitting up in bed chatting with the hospital personnel and me.

After the nurse left, Wendell turned to me and said, "There

are some things we need to talk about." He started rattling off things I would need to do after he was gone, including having an auction to sell his tools and guns.

I didn't want to hear it. It was just too horrible to contemplate. "We can talk about it later. You need to rest."

"No, we need to talk about it now, right now," he insisted gently.

I spent the next hour or so listening to him plan everything from the auction to his cremation, as tears I couldn't hold back slipped down my face. I remember nodding and occasionally choking out something like, "Okay, I understand. I will."

The nurses came to start Wendell's chemotherapy and gave him some medication that made him drowsy. I stayed at his bedside as he slept, my thoughts whirling in a haze of anticipatory grief.

That bizarre discussion about what to do after he died was our last coherent conversation. I didn't fully realize it then, but in just a few more days, grief such as I'd never imagined would shake me to the core, change my life, and change me into someone I could no longer recognize.

The chemotherapy couldn't stand up to the cancer raging through his body, but it had the unwanted effect of causing his liver and kidneys to begin shutting down.

Thus began the end.

PROLOGUE

I 'd been divorced from my first husband, Jack, for several years when I met Wendell Anderson. I was focused on raising my daughter, Kim, and working as a registered nurse at the local hospital in our small Southern Illinois town. I also went back to Southern Illinois University to work on my master's degree in health education.

Wendell and I met in our area Mensa chapter. He grew up in a small town in Central Illinois. After a stint working in Army Intelligence in Japan during the Vietnam War era, he worked his way through Optometry College. When we met, he had an active practice in a nearby town, where he owned a home in the countryside. Besides being intelligent, he had a gentle wit and a quiet air of strength. I liked him. We were friends for several years before he asked me out to dinner—for a Tuesday evening. I couldn't help remarking Tuesday was an odd "date night". "Well, you do eat on Tuesdays, don't you?" Yes, I did, I confessed, and agreed to go. (I found out later Tuesday was his day off, and he wanted the entire day to get ready!) We went to dinner that Tuesday in March, and on June twenty-second we were married. When we got engaged, our mutual Mensa friends were flabbergasted. "You two are so different!" one said. "He's so quiet, and you are so, uh, 'bubbly'". (He meant I was a chatterbox.)

Nevertheless, eleven and a half years later we were happily married when Wendell began to complain of being tired. At that time, the fall of 1997, he was working six days a week at his large optometric practice in Marion, IL, located in one of two Super Wal-Marts in Illinois. We both had learned to SCUBA dive that summer, and we were all set for a trip after Thanksgiving to Grand Cayman to dive in the Caribbean. I thought the trip would give him a chance to rest and relax. When we arrived the weather and the turquoise ocean were gorgeous. I couldn't wait to get in the water! Wendell said he felt too tired to dive safely. However, he insisted I go on all the dives we had pre-scheduled. When I returned from each dive, he listened attentively as I raved about reefs and stingrays and all the underwater marvels I experienced. I secretly speculated that he was intimidated by the ocean. After all, we had only dived in a chilly 60-foot-deep quarry in Illinois, vastly different from the depths of the ocean.

One warm evening we sat on the beach in reclining chairs, holding hands, looking out at boat lights winking on the ocean's horizon. Later that night we made love. I had no idea it would be the last time.

Two days after we got home Wendell told me he felt too sick to go to work. Two days later he was in our local hospital, and two days after that he was transferred by ambulance to an oncology unit at Barnes Hospital in St. Louis, MO. Kim and her husband, Ron, drove me to the Barnes Annex, a hotel-like complex for families of Barnes patients. A complimentary shuttle took me back and forth from the Annex to the hospital, where each day the news was more and more grim.

"It's melanoma." "It has metastasized to his liver." "We're going to try chemotherapy to buy him some time." "The chemo has caused his liver and kidneys to fail." "There's nothing more we can do. You can take him home. We recommend hospice."

The perceptive, compassionate woman who was his primary oncologist took me aside in the hall. "I know you're a nurse," she said. "By the time he began to complain of feeling tired, it was already in his liver. There was nothing to be done, even if you had got him here sooner. Please don't blame yourself." She saved me from a lifetime of guilt.

Kim and Ron drove up Saturday in our van and took us back home to the yellow two-story house Wendell loved so much. Ron virtually carried him into the house to the hospital bed TIP of Illinois Hospice had set up in our living room. Kim and Ron stayed, sleeping in our bed upstairs. I slept on the living room couch. Wendell slipped into a coma Sunday evening. On Monday, my mother and my dear friend and fellow VA nurse, Doris Frye, came to be with us. Wendell died at 1 am Tuesday, December twenty-third. He had been "sick" for two weeks.

A few weeks after Wendell's death I began writing in a blank journal book someone gave me. I didn't write every day, just when I felt the need. Although not planned, the journal's last page was filled a year and a day after he died.

Throughout the years I re-read the journal several times. Each reading found me further along in my grief resolution. In 2021 I re-read the journal as I was packing books into boxes in preparation for the installation of new carpet in my apartment. It struck me once again, if I'd had something like this to read at the time, when my grief was fresh, it could have helped and comforted me. This time I decided to act on that insight.

Except for a few comments in italics for clarification, these journal entries are just as I wrote them, stream of thought, imperfect punctuation and all.

THE FIRST YEAR: COPING WITH WIDOWHOOD

January 22, 1998.

It's been 4 weeks and 1 day—a month tomorrow. I hurt more now than I did 2 weeks ago—or was I just too numb I couldn't feel it yet, or just didn't believe it was real? I don't know. I don't care. I just hurt so bad. I miss him so much. Just now I played that stupid game on the computer. It distracted me for a while, until I remembered how he would come in here and stand behind me as I sat at the computer. He would rub my neck and shoulders for a few minutes, then sometimes he'd say, "Come to bed." Or he'd just go ahead in and read. Sometimes he'd pull up the other chair and say something he wanted to discuss. "Can I put this in your computer?" We knew each other so well. It took years, though. I miss the intimacy, the shared smiles, unspoken jokes, everything that took more than 11 years to build. I don't know if I'll ever have the energy to build a life with someone else like that again. So much give and take. So much to learn. So much of myself to invest. I would want to, but I don't know if I can.

The house is almost the way I always thought I wanted it to be—clean, tidy, not much dust, everything put away in an organized—more or less—way. Now that it's almost "perfect", I know it will never be perfect enough to replace him. I yearn for the clutter next to the bed and on the dresser. I ache for the extra laundry and the muddy shoes.

It will be worse after the sale. I know I have to do it—he wanted me to, and what can I do with all that stuff? It's at risk to be stolen and it's a fire hazard, etc. But I will be in bad shape the day of the sale, I can already feel it 2 months away. Selling his beloved tools, his tractor, his other "toys"—the things he garnered over years of auctions and shopping and hoarding. It will be like losing him all over again. Yet in a paradoxical way it hurts to see all those things—the Gravely mowers left where he parked them when he ran the gas out, just 2 months ago or less.

Everything was 2 months ago or less. That is such a short time—yet my life was ripped apart and my heart broken. That's no idle turn of phrase—a broken heart. I feel as if I'm broken and the place where it hurts is in my chest.

Maybe this isn't going to help, to write down how I feel. I can't stop weeping. Sometimes I think I'm just feeling sorry for myself and that "if I really wanted to" I could just pick up and go on. I don't know why I think that sometimes. I obviously can't pick up and go on. I tried at work and was OK for a few days and then suddenly it was not OK. I had no energy or will to do anything. I wanted to come home, to be home. When I'm here, sometimes I don't want to leave. But when I leave I can't wait to get back. I feel safer here. Outside, I don't know when the tears will come. I get embarrassed. I don't want strangers to see me cry. I don't want to explain.

I can't understand clearly why I'm in such a rush to get a security system put in. Oh, it's logical, rational, etc. I'll be safer, from burglary, fire, etc. But I never felt threatened before. We never even locked our doors most of the time. I was often alone if Wendell worked or went to a sale. It's as though by dying he stripped away my safety net, left me vulnerable to all manner of bad things.

I know he didn't want to die, didn't mean to. We had so many plans, so much to look forward to. I don't "blame him" and I don't feel anger at him for leaving me. Yet, at the same time I do feel abandoned. I feel something "unfair" has happened. There was no time to prepare. No time to ask questions, to find out practical things.

I guess I'll be OK money wise. I'm spending some to finish the basement and I got the new sweeper. But after the security system and motion sensor lights are in, that's enough. I thought about new carpet downstairs but it's too soon. I want to see if I can manage routine expenses on my salary and the rent houses income. I should try to sit down and figure up expenses, but I can't seem to garner the energy or will to do that. Energy is a strange thing. I can do a lot of physical things—vacuum, wash curtains, pull up the old *(basement)* carpet, carry boxes out to the barn and so on. It's the mental stuff that wears me out. I can't think properly. I have trouble with decisions.

Jenny *(kitten)* is here helping me. She's such a comfort. Wendell was fond of her and was her rescuer, gave her her precious name *(Jenny Anydots)* which is so suited to her.

January 23

One month today. N from TIP Hospice came over today. She was kind and understanding about how I feel about returning to work. She suggested if I have the time coming, which I do, to take another 4 weeks leave of absence. I made an appointment to see Dr. H Tuesday to see if he agrees and will "recommend" it. She asked if I felt I needed any medication. I don't think I do. I think I just need time away from work to get more things at home settled and be able to focus more. I can't "give" yet to anyone else and that job requires a lot of giving, plus the stress of the place itself is incredible now. Perhaps it will only get worse but I just cannot deal with it—I found that out Weds.

I did some number crunching this afternoon. If I had to I could liquidate everything, buy a small house somewhere and live modestly without ever working again. That's not what I want. But it's somehow a comfort to know I could if I needed to. Just for the "fun" of it, I may check the want ads to see what's out there. I could take a different job at half the salary I have now and manage very well. No elaborate vacations or entertaining, and again that's not what I want. But it's valuable to me to realize I have options. The only option I don't have is to have Wendell back. It just occurred to me that I haven't cried since N left. Perhaps deciding to stay home a while has reduced some internal pressure. I hope Dr. H will see it that way.

Sunday Jan. 25

The sun is shining today. It helps. I've puttered about. Stripped up some linoleum. Bagged up the trash. Cleaned the bird cage. Called Wendell's folks. (That's hard but I feel close to him when I call them.) Took a load of stuff to garage and pole barn and did a little tidying in the garage.

Naprosyn didn't come in the mail from Wal-Mart. I guess I'll have to go in there tomorrow. I hate it. It tears me up and I hate losing control in public. At home I can just let it come. When I'm somewhere else, I hate that people see. I don't really care what they think. I just hate it when it happens.

I'm wondering what Dr. H will say to me. I'm concerned he may either suggest I try going back to work soon or try to prescribe something for my "nerves". I'm not nervous. I just can't function at work and for now I don't want to try. I want to rest my brain and do physical things—clean house, walk the dog.

Tomorrow night is the car class at John A. *(John A. Logan Community College, adult education course)* I'll go because I think I need to. Same with the gun class on Tuesday.

Kim will probably stay all night tonight. It's somehow comforting to have her here.

Spoke with Andrew *(one of my nephews in Texas)* last night. He and Susan are divorcing. He sounds OK, less pompous than usual. Maybe he'll be OK. I think he's a little jealous of Patrick's *(his brother)* move up here.

Feb 3

Six weeks today. I would write—this moment, this second—that I'm feeling better—but in 10 minutes I may feel terrible again. Yet it does seem to be easing up a little. I told Z it feels like I'm carrying a tremendous heavy "something", weighing down my shoulders, making me tired—and I can never seem to put it down, even for an instant. How I long to just lay this thing down for an hour, a day, to feel "normal" whatever that is. I guess I want to feel like I used to feel when Wendell was here. So, what I'm saying is I want him here. Since that is obviously not possible, it creates a sense of frustration and being trapped in an existence I didn't want, didn't ask for, didn't "deserve". Rationally, I know this is not a matter of asking or deserving or any of that. As C. S. Lewis says, I have joined the countless legions of the grieving—mine isn't unique, except to me. All this philosophical consideration doesn't change the fact of the pain—how I hurt, hurt, hurt. It's visceral and it bends me over sometimes. Other times I just weep. Perhaps the periods of weeping are becoming shorter. I can get control quicker. I did manage to get groceries the other day without weeping at the crème horns and sweet rolls.

Sunday I told Wendell's mother I would make arrangements for his ashes to be sent up there if they wanted to bury him in the family plot. She wept and seemed grateful. I told her I probably would not come often and would not come for a memorial service if they had one. Maybe I would but I really don't want to. She may think me callous and unfeeling. No matter. I loved him so much. I cannot think of him as "in the ground" in any place. He is all around me in this house.

Even though I will sell many things and have given others away, I will keep many things to remind me. Even if I kept nothing, he's with me all the time. I speak to him as though he could hear me. The other day I even fussed at him about something. No matter. I must need to do these things or I wouldn't do them. Even now I weep quietly, for him, for myself, for the grayness of the day, and the yawning hole in my life that only barely begins to show signs of filling in to keep me from tumbling through it.

Feb 13 Friday—

Seven and ½ weeks. Is it really getting easier or is it just the medicine? I try not to think about going back to work. Business as usual. Except there is no more usual. Nothing is usual anymore.

Patrick *(my 37-year-old nephew from Texas, whom I invited to live here in the apartment on the back of the property)* will be here Monday. I think that will be good. It will be a distraction anyway.

I'm learning to shoot the gun. Even considering buying a revolver to keep on the first floor. What a change.

The basement carpet will be in by end of Sunday. If the sweeper is repaired and returned I can get the house the way I want it on Monday and Tuesday. Basically, clean and things in order. I got more gravel for the driveway, but I don't think I want to do anything else to the house for a while. Maybe in a year or two I'll get new carpet—I don't know. Why am I rambling on about carpet and gravel? Why can't I think about my feelings about Wendell? I miss him. It still hurts. It's like putting my tongue into a sore tooth to think consciously of him. Gone. I will never see him again. So fast. So fast. Not enough time to talk, to hold him.

Sunday March 1

I've lost track of the number of weeks. It's about 10 I think. The pain comes at odd times and often at night, after I turn out the light. The bed is still large and feels empty, but a little less so.

Going to the Unitarian Church with Z has been a positive experience. I wish I could share it with Wendell. I miss that so much, being able to share a tale or a joke or something important with him. It's as though I'm cut off, cut in half. Some things are only "half there", half experienced.

Why am I eating more than I should? Am I trying to console myself with food? I know it won't work and only brings me pain, physical and emotional. Why do I still do it?

I slept 11 hours last night and probably could have slept more. I felt better when I got up than I did last night. I thought perhaps I was catching a cold.

Mensa was yesterday. I had planned to go but at the last minute I didn't want to. Not certain why. I watched a movie I'd seen before and later ate chili with Patrick, then I went to bed early. I'm just not ready to see the Mensa group yet.

I went back and read this book from the beginning. I'm no C.S. Lewis, but at least I am able to get some of my pain down on paper.

Yesterday I saw a financial planner. I gave him some basic info and he assures me if I want to, I can retire in 2 ½ years at 55. To walk away from the VA seems like a good thing now, but it would be a great challenge. I would need a plan, something else to bring in some money possibly. I would miss some people from VA, P, F, R and others, but I'm certain I will make new friends by then. I suppose it's possible I could even meet a man to love by then. I must be very careful in that area.

Weds March 4

This evening after work K met me at The Refuge for coffee. She lost her husband 8 yrs. ago. It was a great relief to talk with someone near my age who has been there, is there. She listened non-judgmentally and validated all my feelings. She told me she came back to work a week after her husband died, but she said it was too soon and she never properly resolved her grief. She was so kind, so caring. It was truly good to talk with her. She said it helps her when she can help someone else.

It's 10 weeks now. The time passes. Some days are so long, others shorter. I guess it's always been that way. It's just that the longer ones weren't so filled with pain before.

I'm starting to dread the auction. It's 2 weeks from Sat. It will be a sort of milestone, a closure, yet thinking of all Wendell's precious tools and "toys" going hurts so much it makes me ill. The longer I wait, though, the worse it would be, I think. Better to do it now and get the hurt behind me.

Tomorrow is Mom's birthday. Kim and I are taking her to dinner. Patrick has to work. Thank God her health is holding. I would suffer so to lose her soon. Wendell was supposed to be here to help me through that when the time comes.

Funny things, habits and routines. I told K I don't have my routines anymore but that's not quite true. I fool with the computer game, come to bed, listen to the jazz (new habit), read or write til I'm sleepy, then sleep. Hopefully, getting up to go to work will be a routine. It isn't yet, not quite.

Breakfast is lonely—it was the only meal we always had together. Now I have to hard boil eggs to keep them from going bad. I can't get used to anything in the context of one. I could travel anywhere I wanted—I usually went alone. But no place beckons me. I'd like to dive again, but I need to get in better shape. I wish T hadn't stopped teaching the water aerobics class. The new girl is poor.

Finally tired enough to sleep.

Monday, March 9, 1998

Eleven weeks tomorrow. The auction is less than 2 weeks away. I'm dreading it.

Bad weekend. Friday night terrible. Couldn't sleep, cried and cried until I was exhausted. Then dreams, vivid. I thought I was awake. Wendell was there. I kept touching him, holding him, hugging him and saying, "I can feel you. You're really here, I'm not asleep, I'm not dreaming." And I said, "Do you know how much I love you?" And he said, " Yes, I do." That's the last thing I remember before I woke up, feeling bad. I think because it had been so "real". It scared me to think I couldn't tell the difference between being awake and asleep and dreaming. Was depressed all morning. Finally did some physical stuff, cleaning out gutter and vacuuming and felt a little better. The kids *(Kim and Ron)* came over Sat. evening which helped. I don't even want to think about their going to Florida. Maybe it won't happen.

I heard somewhere—again—that if a woman is single at age 30 chances are she will not marry. I defied those statistics once by remarrying at 40. Odds are it won't happen again. (I'm also pickier than I was at 40, for various reasons.) Even so, the idea is depressing. I don't like the idea of not being with someone. I need to be aware of this feeling when I make decisions about what I eat and wear, whether or not I exercise, etc. It would be so easy to "let myself go"—easier than dying, but a different kind of death, really. I need to take care of myself. A lot of the time I feel like it's just not worth the effort. Getting fat and sloppy would be a sure ticket to being alone for the rest of my life.

I enjoy going to church with Z. The men there who appear to be single seem dippy so far. I'm sure I will eventually meet some interesting people. (Maybe they think I'm dippy, too.)

Weds. March 18

Two more days until the auction. I can barely stand it. I had to come home early yesterday and take some valium and sleep. I haven't slept well all week. Today was better, but only manageable. I have to do this. Wendell wanted me to do this. He specifically told me to. It's one of the few things he asked me to do. I can't seem to make myself go to Delta *(health club with pool)*. I want to come home, eat supper, watch TV and read and be left more or less alone. I don't think that's a good thing but just now it's all I can handle. I've cried more this week than since January. Why? Maybe I feel as if I'm getting ready to let go of all Wendell's things, his beloved tools, the things he accumulated so painstakingly over the years, cleaned and polished and moved around, and cared for so passionately. It will all be gone in one day.

I've been thinking about the house. I don't know how long I will stay here. If I could find a really nice one-story with a basement and a nice yard, close to town, but perhaps still out a little, I would consider moving in a year or so. I will stay here for now, but I think it will be too much for me to manage.

My head aches quite a bit lately. Probably tension. My memory is still poor and I still can't get up much enthusiasm for work, especially all the Joint Commission panic. In a couple of weeks I'll discuss with Mr. B about possibly retiring at 55. Trouble is, at this point, I don't know what I'd do, even if I had enough income to be comfortable.

Fri. March 20

Tomorrow is the sale. I will be glad when it's over.

Sat. March 21 11:58 pm

It's over. $22, 833.00 Not as much as I would have liked but enough. I don't know how Wendell would feel. I guess it really doesn't matter. I'm even from the $20,000 I gave Kim, so I will have about $150,000 to invest, keeping some back for contingency. Now I have to learn all I can about financial planning. I don't want to make mistakes.

Tues March 24

Hard day. Felt like not going in but I went. Kim called upset because a stray dog had killed her goat. She was nearly hysterical. I left to go to her. It was a reason to leave. Why is it getting harder instead of easier? Or is it really? Am I imagining that I feel worse this week than the week before? Is that "normal"? I seem to have no purpose, no enthusiasm for anything. I do what I must. I don't look forward to things like I used to. The future looms ahead like an empty, dark tunnel. Sometimes I think it would not be so bad to die. Not that I would kill myself, not actively. I just don't seem to be very interested in living. Occasionally I think of something I might want to do, then it seems to take too much effort. I can't seem to stop eating. I obsessed yesterday on chocolate. Why am I doing this to myself? I can feel myself slipping sometimes. Today it occurred to me to quit work BEFORE I'm 55, so, in a few months. Why? I'm only 52. What would I do with myself? I need to try to hang on at least a year. That's what the conventional wisdom is— "Don't do anything drastic for a year." It's as if I know what is happening to me and I can't stop it, even though I tell myself I can. If this goes on much longer I think I'll need to see someone professionally. Perhaps another talk with K would help. I really felt better after I talked with her a few weeks ago. Tonight I wanted to talk to someone but I couldn't think of who to call. I didn't really want " cheered up". I didn't want to impose on anyone or upset anyone, like M. I almost wish I was planning a trip, so I'd have something to look forward to. Perhaps when the kids get settled in Florida I can plan a trip there. However, I'd better quit using up my leave in pieces and bits so I can take a trip when I want to.

Sat. Mar 28

I've been going to bed early lately—can't keep my eyes open. Took a nap this afternoon because I was so tired. Kind of scary. I thought maybe I was sick. Later I had more energy. Cleaned the basement, glued down the tile that has been annoying me for so long, and I did 2 loads of laundry. I didn't eat well today. Kind of snacked and ate bread and butter. Didn't feel like cooking anything. I spend a lot of time playing that computer card game. It's mindless, yet I have to focus. I could be wrong, but it both relaxes me and helps me focus my mind.

Patrick didn't call to let me know if his friends are coming tomorrow or not. I know he doesn't mean to be thoughtless but I need to know if people are coming and what time.

I guess I'll go to church with Z tomorrow. I'm not sure how I feel about that. I enjoy seeing her, but I think in the summer I will find I need Sunday mornings to get things done when it's still cool.

I feel really blah. No energy or enthusiasm. Not as bad as last week though, I think. It's so hard to tell because my feelings change. One minute I'm so low. Then later I "forget" and am distracted by something, and even enjoy doing something for a while and then—low again without warning. I miss him so much. Part of me still can't accept that he is gone. I mean, I really feel him around me, talk to him, catch myself listening for him. Yesterday when I was mowing I kept looking for the truck to come up the driveway. The truck was already parked behind the van but I still kept checking the end of the driveway. I wonder how long I will do that.

N came Thursday and stayed for 2 hrs. She lets me "dump" all my feelings out and draws me out if I get stuck. I know it's her job but I think she's doing it more as a friend.

What to do with my life? What an odd position to be in. It never occurred to me that I would possibly be able to consider not working at this age. Yet, what would I do with my time, especially in the winter? Could I make a hobby of cleaning this house? I could do some repainting, I guess. The office needs it and so does my bedroom. Both rooms need new carpet, too, but I'm not sure if I should do that if I have to move in a year or two. I may need to hang on to the money that new carpet would take.

Thurs. April 2

The mowers both started for me today. I was thrilled. A small victory! I mowed until nearly out of gas and got almost all of it done, including over half of the west side. It's very thick over there and bumpy. It's amazing the things I think about while I mow. Wendell, of course. It's as though I'm mowing it for him again, so he won't have to do it when he comes home. Perhaps as long as I live in this house I will have that sense of his being here. I'm beginning to feel some pressure from within to move and buy a different place, sell this one, etc. I especially feel pressure to quit working. I don't really think I should. I have so much to gain if I can hang on for even a couple more years. Until I'm 55. At least financially anyway.

V left a message inviting me somewhere. I didn't call her back. I didn't feel like going out. Yesterday evening out with B and D was fun but I needed to mow and go to bed early. Stayed up late last night for some reason. Some nights I just can't get settled down, even if I don't cry much. I have these impulses, like I'll call someone to talk—and then I change my mind. I feel mired. Inertia. I just want to stay here, clean, mow, garden, wash the dog, etc. Obviously can't do that for the next 30 years! Time. Time, time, time. Time will help. I'll feel better in time. In time, it will ease, pass, let up, get better, whatever. Time seems to have a different meaning. I was thinking—I can't go back to life like it was before Wendell. I remember eating spaghetti on a tray table in front of the TV in my robe and watching some movie or other. It was safe, I guess. Wendell changed my life so much. How can I go back to that? But how can I go forward? I don't know who or what I am now. I'm re-forming, reshaping my life. I suppose I can be whatever I want, within reason. I just really can't think of a thing. If I quit work tomorrow, what on earth would I do with my time?

Sunday April 5

It seems my life is becoming a series of cliches. "Money can't buy happiness." "Haste makes waste." "What is the meaning of life?"

Right now I feel so isolated. The worst part of losing Wendell—at least as I perceive it at present—is losing my best friend, my soul mate, my alter ego. How I miss talking with him, sharing with him, even arguing with him. When I think I'll never have that sick feeling in the pit of my stomach when he was angry with me over something, I think that part is good. But I'd take that feeling back many times to have him back with it. Those times were fewer and fewer. Our lives were getting better and better. He worked so hard for us to have it all—the house, the grounds, he tools, the trips, the lifestyle we wanted. He got it—and then died before he could really enjoy it. Sometimes I feel so guilty that I will have so much now that he is gone. I don't even have to work if I decide not to. Another cliché—"You have to have money to make money"—and now it seems I have it—am making it.

Maybe after I retire I could write. I always wanted to. I know I can. I just need to discipline myself to do it. I could write what I know—about nursing, or marriage, living with alcoholism, diving, etc. I think I could do that. I could even do a column again for a newspaper or send in articles to a magazine. I might even get paid for writing something. I have all the tools I need, the computer, etc. Z writes professionally and can give me some assistance, contacts, etc. I will think about this.

This journal started out to be my writing out my grief, my feelings about losing Wendell. Maybe it's time to let it become something more. I can "talk to myself" this way, try out ideas, come back to them later to see if they still have value. There is still room for the grief.

Tues Ap 7

Tomorrow I meet with B to set up retirement. As much as I want to get out now, I'd be smart to stay at least 6 months, better a year, best until I'm 55. I checked today and the health insurance will be $221/mo –I think that's the group rate, which I can only keep for 18 months. I can convert to non-group rate then, but it will be higher still. I talked with J about selling the rental houses. I put an ad in the Sou IL for the van. Even if I raise the max from the van and rentals I would probably have to sell this house within a year to maintain cash flow if I quit now. If I can hang on for even a year it will make a big difference, especially if I move some of the TSP $ into C and the market steps up even moderately high. I sure don't depend totally on the market though, so I need to talk to P *(my supervisor)* about helping me set priorities. I can't bring work home. I just can't! She needs to tell me where she wants me to focus my energy.

Yesterday I saw K *(a nurse practitioner)* at Dr. H's. She changed my medication from Prozac to Zoloft. Too soon to tell a difference. I'm sleepy, but who knows?

Storm warnings out tonight. Tornado watch—a warning in effect up by Vandalia. I should have gone over this with Patrick. He's at work now. I don't even know if he understands the sirens or what to do. Surely if he were home, he'd come over here if he realized there was a warning.

I have my radio on, a transistor, extra batteries, flashlights, a map, a magnifier, and clothes laid out in case I need to get dressed and go to the basement in a hurry. If push comes to shove I could sleep in the basement if I had to, since the couch is down there.

Sunday April 12

I have a new puppy. Kim gave him to me as an "early Mother's Day" present. He is 2 mos old and a golden retriever. He is beautiful! His name is Buddy, and he's adorable—and very good. Lori *(our poodle mix dog)* is jealous. In time she'll come around. She needed a companion and I needed something to hug and cherish. He looks at me with such unconditional love in his eyes. It makes me feel good.

I had a cry today. When I pulled back the truck seat to put away a toolbox and found an animal cracker. It cut like a knife and I wept hard for a minute or two. So painful, so unexpected.

I guess I have to try to stay at work. If I leave now or even in the fall, I would almost certainly have to sell the house. When I was adding up what I would need to live on, I forgot to include income tax. Maybe if the kids like it in Florida, I could go there in 2 ½ yrs. Mom? She may be gone by then—who knows? She's doing so well now, but she fell Tuesday—a reminder that it could happen so quickly. She wasn't hurt but could have been. A broken hip or leg would be the beginning of the end, if not the end itself.

To keep my health insurance would cost nearly $2000 a year, as opposed to it coming off my check now and I don't even notice it. Some expenses would go down, but not enough.

The ad is in the paper for the van—but only one nibble so far. I will renew it for one week and add some details, ac, power windows/locks, conversion, tape deck, table, curtains, very nice. Maybe then I'll get some offers. I'd like to sell It myself. If I sell it on consignment, I'll either have to ask more or get less. I want to get $4000 out of it.

Ron says David *(his brother)* can fix the pipe from the sump so it drains closer to the pond. It's a mess out there. I can't mow it. I mowed Sat—the entire yard, west side too, with the Grasshopper, including the whole dam. I had to jump the mower again. I guess I'll need to get a new battery. L said he'd come help me do that on Tuesday. I'll need to take off an hour early if I can to go get a battery. I also need to get some Carmex (? Sp) and spray the pond. The algae is clogging it, including messing up the fountain. It needs done pretty soon. I haven't heard from the pond guy, but I think I can do it myself. I need to get more fish food too. Maybe if I can, I'll leave at 2 on Tuesday to do all that before L gets here at 5.

Tomorrow evening is the dinner for Dr. L at Farris's. I signed up to go and I guess I will. Going there will not be easy. It was special to Wendell and me. Our first date was there and we ate there often until the last year or so. I will try not to think about that and just enjoy the evening the best I can.

April

It seems every day I lose another little piece of you.

Yesterday it was the new checks with only my name.

Today a catalog that said "Last Chance—order now or no more catalogs"—in your name.

Another day an insurance card for the car in just my name.

And it goes on, day by day.

Like an onion, peeling away the layers of our lives until only my life is left.

How long will it be before I lose the feeling of you lying beside me?

How long until I can't recall your face, every scar, every mole?

How long before I stop using phrases you used?

How long before the parrot stops mimicking your voice?

How long before I remember to say "I" instead of "we"?

How long before something breaks down and I don't cry in anguish, "Wendell, why aren't you here?"

How long before I stop needing you?

The only thing I'm sure will never end is that I love you.

Friday April 17

I couldn't go Monday night. Had the blues. Did manage to get the battery and some groceries but couldn't manage going to Farris's. Went Weds for dinner with K. It helps to talk with her. She says it helps her, too. It's been 8 yrs for her. God, I can't even imagine ahead 8 years. Not quite 4 mos and I feel so BAD. Sometimes I'm convinced I'm losing my mind. Can't think, can't focus, can't remember things, lose track in the middle of a sentence. Other times I'm OK, even feel OK, sometimes even feel "good", but it doesn't last. I feel like a yo-yo…up, down, up, down—it's exhausting.

I sit at the computer and play the game. Lately I have also begun to sing as I play, a haunting chanting melody, sometimes without words, sometimes with. The computer hums in a minor key. I don't consciously sing, I just find I'm singing. Sometimes it's an ordinary song, but often an odd, almost oriental or semetic song.

Lost and Found

I lost you.
I looked and you were there.
And then I looked and you were gone.

Sometimes I find you for a moment.
In a picture, in a phrase.

Sometimes I find you in the truck or the garage or in the yard.

Sometimes I find you in a book or in a shirt, or at the store,
in cookies and in crème horns.

Sometimes I find you on the phone or in the mail.

Sometimes I find you when I least expect.

Sometimes I find you in my dreams.

Mon. April 20

Often when we walked

Your longer legs carried you ahead of me.

Sometimes I was annoyed that you left me behind.

What will people think, I said to myself,

That he rushes ahead not thinking of her as she struggles to keep up with him?

Did you notice? Did you really want to go ahead alone? Or could you just not

slow your pace and stride, your rhythm and gait?

Could you not hold back, impatient to be on your way,

In a hurry to arrive, anxious not to miss a moment of what lay ahead?

Once again, you have left me behind to struggle.

Tuesday April 21

Dear Wendell,

I've never done this before, write you a letter. It just occurred to me to do so. I will write as though you will read it, although my mind knows you are beyond sentient thought and communication. As I write tears flows quietly. I miss you so much. I would give much to be able to sit and talk with you and hold you in my arms and have you hold me. The thought that that cannot be is almost more than I can bear. In so many ways you are with me still. You "pop up" all day long, as today in my roll-a-dex and later too with a patient named Wendell. That name will always mean you to me. With Jack I have known dozens of "Jacks" since and I seldom think of him in relation to that name. But the name Wendell is always and forever you for me. Going on without you is the hardest thing I've ever done. Every day is a struggle. I know it as soon as I wake up. The luster is gone from my life just as though a cloud were permanently lodged in front of the sun. Everything is duller, slower, drab and blunted by your absence. When one person goes away on a trip and you miss him, the pain of separation is offset by the anticipation of seeing him again when you are reunited. However, losing you is final and has no hope of reunion. That's not my faith, not my belief. I wish it were, so I could hold the hope of seeing you again. But it will not be. I have you only in my heart, in pictures, and in the thoughts of our family and friends. People continue to be kind to me. It makes me feel fragile, and I guess in some ways I am. I never realized how many things you took care of that I paid so little attention to. Now I am bereft of you and of what you knew and of your help and talent and wit and chuckle and smile, and your tuneless humming and your funny facial expressions and your not so delicate table manners and your stacks of magazines and newsletters and your strength and your patience and your shoes piled on the bedroom floor, and your kindness and your hours in front of the mirror and your funny teasing, claiming to do all the decorating and party preparations, and your sarcasm and rare nasty temper, and your quiet watchful intelligence and your stacks of books and your shoulder to lean on and your backrubs and back scratches and your smell and your salty taste and I am bereft of all of this and I hurt so much. I wish you had not had to die.

(July 20 P.S. I forgive you for dying. I love you.)

Weds. Ap 22

Ways I have dealt with loss in the past:

J and P *(friends who died in high school)*-talked with Jack and my friends

Jack's mother-comforted Jack

Miscarriage-never fully resolved that grief, possibly because I was "disenfranchised" *(felt I was treated as if I were ill, not grieving)*

Loss of job-initial panic, then turn loss into opportunity, went back to school, started a new life, 1 major support person

Divorce-anger, still some unresolved, guilt, dive into new life, new relationship

Grandma-relief, release for her, memories, pictures, buried her in gown I got her

Grandpa-difficult; the funeral director wouldn't let me say goodbye, rushed me—I hated him for years. Lived in their *(my grandparents')* house and judged men by him

Loss of my dad-supported my mom, took comfort from fact he didn't linger and suffer—still grieve for him a lot, or at least I did before every other grief was dwarfed by losing Wendell

A support group for widows—could I do it? Should I do it? Perhaps start small and invite a few friends over-K, A, J, E, L. Would it work? Would I want to devote the time and energy to it? Or would I later want to "drop it" and move on to something else. If I made a commitment to be there for others, could I do it? Sometimes I can barely go on myself. It's too soon to do it now. In 5 or 6 months maybe.

I have to quit eating like I am. Perhaps if I try to understand why. Am I bored? Feeling guilty? Trying to build a "defense" of ugliness to avoid possible future entanglements?

I'm so tired. I'm sleepy, yes, but the tiredness is more. I'm doing the work of living that 2 people were doing before, besides the general exhaustion from the grief itself. It's like having my batteries drained and never fully recharged. Everything is such a chore. I do stuff but there is no delight, no real joy.

What will I do when Kim goes to Florida? 2 years! (The plan was to stay for 2 years.) Why did that have to happen now? I will really miss her terribly. I'm afraid she will miss me too. I will worry about her. Ron is basically good to her but he's insensitive to some of her needs. I try not to think of her going.

I need to sleep.

Thurs. Ap 23

Before you, I was.

With you, I was more.

Without you, I can be again.

But when?

When will I feel whole again?

When will I no longer feel like half of something else?

How long before I'm "me" again instead of part of "we"?

How long before I learn to say "my house", "my car", "my anything" instead of "ours"?

How long before the "we" dies like you did?

How soon do I begin to feel like getting up and living?

How long before the world feels "normal"," right", or "safe"?

When will I have energy for anything but tears without great effort?

Only tears come easily now.

4 months today. 1/3 of a year. When 2 times this much time has passed it will be one year. How can time go fast and slow all at once? In some ways it seems like it happened a lifetime ago. In other ways it's as if I live it over and over and it's immediate, at least it feels like fresh pain. Everyone tells me how well I'm doing. Because I can get up, bathe, dress, go to work, come home, mow lawn, do laundry, go out, go to church, buy groceries, pay bills, answer the phone, go to the dentist, watch TV, read a book, clean my gun, put gas in the car—all this stuff sounds so "normal". The problem is none of it is normal. Everything is in sepia tones instead of technicolor. Everything is an effort. Nothing comes easy— except crying, which I can do any time, without warning, until I'm exhausted. If it's "healthy" to get your feelings out then I should be healthy all right. Damn, I'm so sick and tired of feeling sad…I want some joy in my life. I want something to be happy about, to be excited about.

Weds. Ap 29, 1998

Tomorrow is the end of April. It's rained the past 3 days and some on Sunday, too. Don't know for sure, but I think I feel better on sunny days. I wish I knew what I did feel like without any Zoloft or Prozac, but I'm sort of afraid to try yet. Tonight started out badly and ended up OK. For some reason I decided to stop feeling sorry for myself and get up and do something. So I changed the hall bulb that's been out for a week and vacuumed the upstairs, which was way overdue. Perhaps tomorrow I'll vac downstairs. I didn't bring Buddy in, but I should tomorrow.

I ordered a couple of things from a catalog today. Perhaps I should do that once a week or so. It will give me something to look forward to. I wonder if that's why Wendell was so fond of catalogs.

The young couple hasn't called about the van. I hope they buy it. It's in the way and I'd prefer to have the money to invest. I wonder if they can raise the cash. I don't want to have them making payments. Too risky.

All of a sudden I've got the blues. God, I hate this roller coaster feelings stuff. I never really feel "good", but I go from OK to down in the dumps without warning. I definitely need to plan something positive to look forward to. Maybe I'll look into the trip to Florida. I could fly to Kim's, then we could drive to Ft. Lauderdale and do the vacation cruise and drive back to Crestview. I'll probably need to put it off until late fall. I think I'll want to go there for a few days in August or so to help her get settled in. I don't know how I will deal with her being that far away. I have refused to think about it until now. We've never been further apart than from Harrisburg to Carbondale *(just a few miles)* when she was in school and before we moved to Carterville. I know it will be hard for me, but it will be hard for her too.

Mom is getting more frail. I expect her to give up her volunteer work later this year. That will be hard but her balance is so poor—unless this ear thing can be treated, it's dangerous for her to move around without the walker. Hang on, Mom. I can't lose all of you in a single year.

Sat May 2, 1998

Sometimes the kindness of people blows me away. I got the big mower stuck in the ditch. B, our neighbor, and a total stranger who stopped to help got me out. I can do a lot of things but when some things happen I need help. It always seems to be there. So far I've been lucky. P commented on seeing me mowing and offered the use of his trailer if I ever need to get the Grasshopper in for service.

I haven't really had a totally bad day or night this week. I doubled the Zoloft dose to the prescribed level once I realized the sample I'd been given was only 50 mg. instead of the 100 she prescribed. Maybe that's helping. I don't know what I'd feel like without the Rx. I hate to think. I wish I could try it but I'm afraid to. I need my energy level up for work and for work at home. It took me 5 hrs. to mow today, counting the half hr I was stuck. I did the whole place, including the back yard. I tried to get the trimmer going but I flooded it. If it's not raining I'll try tomorrow.

Maybe tomorrow I'll order something from the Vermont Country Store catalog. A summer outfit, maybe. It will give me something to look forward to.

I have to go to the grocery store and write some checks and fix strawberries to take to work for a party.

I told Z I didn't want to go to church tomorrow. I'm not sure how I feel about it. I think if I go, I should take my own car so I can leave when it's over. Easter Sunday they stayed and talked for a half hr. I don't much enjoy that at this point.

Why don't I miss you today as painfully as yesterday?

How can 24 hrs make a difference?

Especially since I suspect that tomorrow I may miss you more than yesterday.

What is it that titrates my grief level?

Does it depend on hormones, weather—clouds, or sun or rain?

Does it depend on whether I'm at home or work?

What force determines how much pain I feel at any given time?

Is it pills or sleep or other thoughts and plans?

If I could plan my grief it would be easier,

Instead of being caught off guard by unexpected pain.

If I could have it all in several hrs a week events and then be sure I'd feel no grief the other days.

I could go and do and know I wouldn't cry.

Tues May 5

Tonight I went to Van Natta's Funeral Home because B's daughter died. It felt strange. I felt detached, not upset as I expected to. I'm certain it's the Zoloft. I don't know which is scarier—wondering what I'd feel like if I didn't take it or continuing to take it because I'm afraid to find out. When Daddy died I couldn't go to Van Natta's for years without getting upset. By rights I shouldn't have been able to get near the place. As it was I drove in, parked, and went in almost in a trance. How long do I want to go on with my genuine emotions masked like this? How long will I have to depend on the pills? Will I be able to cope without them? Should I try to or wait for the Dr. to suggest it? I don't want to be depressed but I hate depending on the pills. I feel like my life isn't real somehow. I'm afraid if I stop taking them and my energy level drops I'll gain more weight and be too tired to do anything. Deadlines are starting to loom at work. After JCAHO is over and I see how that goes, perhaps I'll cut the dose back to 50 mg and then wait a few weeks and see how I feel.

I haven't talked to K lately . I saw the ad in the paper for the "Young Widowed" group—would 52 qualify as "young"? It seems like it to me. I'll try to remember to get the phone # in the morning and call to get info. I guess that gets me off the hook of the idea of starting a group. I thought maybe I could but I'm really not up to it.

Thurs May 7

J called today. I won't get as much for the houses as I had hoped. He says I'll be lucky to get $22,000 each. Wendell paid $25,000 for the Marion house. Of course, it's pure profit minus the capital gains tax. The loss on the Marion house will help offset the gain on the other one. I'm not sure what the purchase price was for the Herrin house but I think it was much lower. Hopefully I'll end up with $36,000 or so to invest. I think I can manage without the income from the houses. I'm able to keep a steady $5-6 thousand in my checking account. The amt in the SIU credit union is nearly $3 thousand and I can use it to pay the real estate taxes. If I sell the van for $3500 that would also pay the taxes.

Tomorrow night B and M and D and I are going to the Hideout for supper at 6. I'm going to try to get to Delta at 4:30 first. I've got to get back there. I'm going to pot! I don't get any exercise and I'm eating the wrong stuff—comfort food, mostly. I do OK at breakfast and lunch but supper is a mess.

Sat I have to take Buddy to the vet and go to the bank and mow. Then Kim and Ron are coming for supper. If it's nice I'll pick up some steaks and grill out. Sounds pretty normal to me. That's the thing I'm worried about. If it's the pills "allowing" me to feel this way, what happens when I quit taking them? What's really going on inside my head? At least they kept me at work. I was not prepared to quit, emotionally or financially. I just couldn't think of staying in March and early April—I wanted out of the "rat race". Trouble is I have no other plan. Maybe it's too soon to have a plan.

Other than traveling, there's nothing I really have a passion for. Traveling takes money so if I want to travel I'd better stay at work and let my nest egg grow. I wish I felt more like doing stuff in the evening. I could clean, do laundry, sew/mend, iron, pay bills, balance my checkbook, etc. but all I want to do lately is eat supper, watch TV a while and to play the computer game until my eyes are bleary. Then I read a while until I can't stay awake. I wonder if I planned one task each evening if that would help.

Spring, 1986
Wendell and I went to Garden of the Gods
Illinois State Park

Wendell and I making our vows
June 22, 1986

My Mom and Dad and Wendell and I
on our wedding Day
June 22, 1986

My brand new husband with my
"something blue" garter"

Halloween was"our thing"
and we gave great parties

Wendell meeting Sam Walton
at Marion, Illinois Walmart Optical
circa 1991

My Mom at our hospital volunteer desk.
1995

Portrait we had done
June, 1997

The Yellow House

My original journal

Mon May 18

So strange. I feel OK for an hour, then awful for an hour, then good for an hour, then exhausted for an hour, then sick for an hour, then scared for an hour, then mad, then frustrated, then sad, then sleepy, then bored, then excited... and so it goes. I'm on a rollercoaster, with more downs than ups and it's a big loop—no progress, or is there, and I just can't see it? In a few days it will be 5 months. How can it seem like a long time yet only yesterday at the same time? Sometimes I can barely remember and other times he is so fresh in my mind that I ache with the knowing that I'll never see him again.

His parents sent a picture of the tomb stone. It hurt.

Tues May 26, 1998

5 month anniversary came and went. The next milestone will be our anniversary on June 22, then 6 months on the 23, and Father's Day is also that week. Maybe I'll take 10 Benadryl and sleep for 3 days and wake up when it's all over.

There's just no zest in my life. How can I pretend everything is good when it's not? I know I'm lucky compared to some. Moles in my yard and 1 car out of 3 that won't run are my worst problems. I guess unless I'm sick. I keep thinking I shouldn't be this tired. I have diarrhea and a stomachache so much. I'm probably exaggerating but I wonder if I could be ill. Somehow the prospect doesn't upset me too much. If I died, Kim would be well off and have no financial worries. It's not that I <u>want</u> to die—it's just that living doesn't interest me much. I've lost my center, my reason for being. I have no goals except to get through a day. Even the prospect of a dive trip to the Bahamas makes me tired to think of it. I've thought perhaps I'd take a trip somewhere, but none of the places I've always wanted to go seem interesting to me now. I had to really make myself go to work today and then I had to make myself stay the whole 8 hrs. It's not that work is bad. I just had trouble concentrating and wanted to go home.

Kim is coming for supper tomorrow. She will move in in a few weeks for a month until they are ready to go to Florida, providing they have a buyer for their land. It's only 6 weeks until they go. It's really bothering me but I don't want her to know it.

I didn't call Wendell's folks this weekend. I just couldn't. It was not kind of me. I'm sure Memorial Day was hard for them too.

June 23

Just when I thought I was doing OK. Yesterday came. Our anniversary. I knew it would be hard. Most of the day wasn't too bad but I was pushing down my pain. When I pinched my thumb in the door I started to cry and I couldn't stop. I woke up this morning crying and I still can't stop. I can't go in to work. It's 6 months today. I'm reading a lot of books on grief. I'm beginning to realize that I have a lot of anger in me. Even though my intellect tells me Wendell didn't die on purpose, the fact remains—he left me. And I'm angry at him for it. I want him to have fought harder, to have sought medical help sooner, anything to have changed this outcome. He left me—and he had no pain! All the pain is here now, in me! It's not fair. He's "at rest" and I'm the one who is suffering. I hate having my life torn apart like this. I hate having all these birds and cats *(Kim's pets)* in the house. My own cats can't go to their food bowls and litter boxes. I'm mad at myself for feeling this way because when the birds and cats are gone it means Kim and Ron are gone. We talk about my going down there but I know I won't go very often and she won't make the trip up here either very often. I was just reading in a book on grief that someone said he wished his friends and family would stop trying to "fix him" and just let him be a mess until he didn't need to be a mess anymore. That's what I am today—a mess—and if I need to be a mess the rest of the day, I'm going to be one. Keeping all this in won't help. If I am to go back to work and function I've got to let off some of the pressure.

Why did I put up such a front to F the hospice SW *(Social Worker)* yesterday? She came to see how I was doing and help me if I needed it. Instead I chatted with her and showed her the birds and told her how well I was doing. Bullshit! If it wasn't for M on the internet, no one would know how I really feel. What I'd really like to do is put my head in someone's lap and cry my heart out—but I don't want to upset anyone. I'm not sure if even Z could handle it. I know Mom can't. I don't think Kim can.

One of my most painful memories is when Doris woke me up because she knew Wendell was dying. I said, "I don't want to wake up." I didn't mean I wanted more sleep. I meant I knew instantly why she was waking me up and I knew if I woke up it would happen and if I didn't wake up I wouldn't have to face it. I've played that scene over and over in my mind. I also feel guilty because I fell asleep. I know I was exhausted but I gave up the last hrs. of his life, of being with him to someone else while I slept. I should have been the one sitting the vigil.

Helplessness. The state of being without help. No help. No help for the chores, the yard, the finances, the future. No way of being of help—no way I could make him stronger, take away the toxins that robbed him of his mind the last few days. No way I could stop the freight train of melanoma that bore down on him—on us. I was like a straw in the wind, an umbrella against the hurricane. I was helpless. Sometimes I still feel helpless.

I called to tell P *(my office assistant)* I wasn't coming in today. She said, "Everybody is looking for you." Even if they were I wish she hadn't said that. I'm trying hard not to feel guilty about not going today. I feel I need an emotional breather and one day wasn't enough, especially since I spent most of it pretending I was in such good shape. How do I tell people that can't possibly understand? They need me to be like I was—and I'm not. I won't be for a long time, maybe never. I'll be better—I've already been better—but today I'm not "better"—today I'm in pain and I just need to go with it. The ones who are looking for me will probably find me tomorrow. If they are frustrated or angry that I'm not there, it's their problem, not mine.

Same day, late evening. I slept a lot today and I think I'll be able to go to work OK tomorrow.

Sent a long note to M. I'm printing them out and will eventually put them with this journal. *(The printouts were misplaced, and I never found them.)* P said everybody was looking for me today. I hope they were patient. I don't want to react irritably to anyone but I don't want to hear anything like "You need to get on with it", etc. They really don't understand. P said she thinks she understands but she doesn't. Losing her dad and mother at an advanced age is sad but it's a different sort of grief—I know from losing Daddy. She just wants to help but she can't really understand. All I need from her is patience.

June 29

June is nearly over. I am starting my 7th month alone, without Wendell. Today it's OK. Tomorrow, who knows?

Kim and Ron were treating me like a senile old woman Sat. It made me mad. Maybe I worry that is what I will become, so that is why it made me so mad.

Nice evening Friday at a musical comedy with Z and L. It felt good to laugh and clap. Sunday night I took everyone out to supper. An extravagance perhaps, but who knows how often we will ever get to do that again?

After Kim and Ron go I hope I can find someone to dive with.

July 2

It's very odd to feel good and bad at the same time. I feel TERRIBLE that Kim is moving so far away next week, but I'll be SO GLAD to get rid of the cats, birds, and dog. I will miss her so much but I want my house back, clean and tidy. I want to eat what I want, when I want, and I want to be able to have my radio and clock in my kitchen. *(Kim was using them in the basement where they were sleeping.)*

I am beginning to think of remodeling the kitchen but won't do anything until next winter/spring—just plan and think about it.

Off and on I miss Wendell so painfully, but now and then I think what would have happened if he were here now? He would not have been able to tolerate Patrick, let alone Kim and Ron and the menagerie. I can barely stand it myself, and he was much less tolerant of that sort of thing. He'd have moved out to a motel! And I would have been upset, guilty, etc. Awful—

What shall I do about Patrick? He seems totally immune to hints. He outright agrees he should be helping me now—and then doesn't. He runs a few errands here and there for me, helpful, but nothing I couldn't do myself—and that's it! He eats here 2 or 3 times a week and contributes no money for food. He occasionally puts gas in the truck—but then leaves it on empty. He picks up the gas in the cans for me, but doesn't offer to pay for it or help me mow. He puts his trash out with mine but doesn't offer to kick in on the trash bill. Granted, he usually only has 1 bag or so—but he doesn't even offer to take mine down as he takes his! Why am I such a wimp? Am I afraid for him to go if I say anything to him? (Of course, he'd be nuts to move out just because he got mad—he's got it made here!) He has a $70 light bill and his gas to and from work—eats breakfast out most mornings—often parties after work. No other bills, except what he puts on his credit card. He watches my satellite TV and uses my VCR. I pay his water bill (granted, it's not that much extra) but he still hasn't <u>offered.</u> It's like the more he gets, the more he takes. If I acted on my old saying, "If you always do what you've always done, you'll always get what you've always got," then I'd change what I'm doing to change what I'm getting, and I'd stop being a doormat . But I hate confrontation. I guess I'd rather be taken advantage of than to confront him. If I had realized how selfish he was, I would never have suggested he move here, regardless of how alone I'd be. I would be frightened if he weren't on the place but I'd get used to it. What in the world will I do if I ever date again? How can I keep him from just "walking in"? Oh, well, I'm tired of bitching about it to myself. Put up or shut up.

Is it my imagination that I feel better this week? Is it just a temporary "up" after last week's big "down"?

I'm beginning to wonder about the pictures. I didn't realize how many there were—the big one in the dining room, the 5 x 7's on the buffet, the wedding pictures and bouquet in the china cabinet—oh, that hurt to think of moving those out. Not ready for that—but up to now it wouldn't have even occurred to me. Also pictures on my desk, on the bedroom desk, and on the jewelry case. Pictures of his mom and dad downstairs, too. That's another kettle of fish. They're starting to make noises like I should come up there. I don't want to. I don't want to see any of them, not even at Christmas. I don't even want to send presents. How do I deal with that? They are hanging onto him by clinging to me.

I'd like to talk to M to see how she's doing. I should send her a card. She's had a rough time, too.

The widow support group is next Tues—I don't know if I'll go, since it's the kids' last week here. Perhaps I'll go for a little while. I wish there were more younger women in it.

I also need to call J.

July 4

I'm writing in the early morning—unusual, but I'm awake and I don't think the kids are up yet. It's raining—hope that won't mess up our plan to cook outside.

In five more days they will be gone. It's so hard but I'm trying to not show them how upset I am at their leaving. I got angry at Ron yesterday for criticizing my drawing. He doesn't have a clue how much that hurts me—and it does no good. He thought I was attacking him and said I couldn't take constructive criticism. I'm sure that is correct—but what he was doing at the time was not constructive, and I worry about Kim. If he leaves her, I don't know if she could make it on her own. Her self-esteem is so low and sometimes Ron makes it worse by teasing her cruelly. Between worrying about her and Mom, it's a burden I wish I didn't have just now. If they were moving a year from now, I could probably take it in stride. Mom's dizzy spells are making it very hard for her to get out and do anything and she's scared she'll fall. Aunt R died yesterday, after falling and breaking her hip—blood clot. Scary—and I know Mom is scared. I wonder if her dizzy spells could be stress related.

July 11

Kim is gone and I can't seem to stop crying. I miss her so much. How can I be there for her if she needs me? She wants me to come down in August. I don't know if I can manage it. I know I'll see her in Sept when we go to Nassau, but that is so long off. I'm so tired. I mowed a little today, then slept for 4 hours. I watched a couple of movies and ate too much. I can't do this to myself but I don't know how to stop. I don't mean to be angry with her but how could she leave me now? It's not reasonable, I know, but I needed her to stay. In a year I could have handled it better—but this was their year, their time, and they had to go. I hope it works out for them. What kind of life can I make for myself? I don't want to be "Patrick's Aunt" or "Kim's Mom who comes to visit"—I want my own life.

I wish that damn black cat would come out so I could not worry about it dying up in the ceiling. *(One of Kim and Ron's cats got up in the ceiling tiles in the basement. They couldn't get her out and had to leave without her!)*

Monday, July 20

Sometimes it hits me hard again that Wendell is really gone. He was so strong, so smart, my tower of strength. I think I just assumed he'd always be here for me so strongly that even "knowing" he's dead leaves me unable to comprehend that he's never coming back. Maybe it's because we were apart so much of the time and came together at night, that bedtime is the hardest. He was always there, piled up in bed reading or already asleep when I came to bed. He was just there –I was safe and not alone. Even if he didn't wake up, I knew he was there for me. Sometimes he'd barely wake up and reach over and "pinch my butt" and sometimes giggle, and go back to sleep. Just knowing he was there made me feel so safe—I didn't know I felt safe until I didn't feel safe anymore. I will never really be safe again. Even if there is eventually someone else lying next to me, I'll always know that he could be snatched away any time. There is no safety, no security. It's a myth. It's only relative. You can go out and take risks, go out of your way to get in harm's way, be stupid or careless, drive too fast, smoke, take chances, etc. Obviously if you do all that you are "less safe" than if you don't. But even if you stay in, never take a known risk, surround yourself with people, lock your doors, buy a gun, etc. you are still not "safe", just less unsafe than before. Being alive is being at risk to die. It's most of the time no one's "fault", no one is to blame. That's just the way it is. The idea is to balance the relative safety with the risk of doing things, meeting people, going places, enjoying what you do.

Before I fell in love with Wendell I had decided I would probably never remarry and had decided to enjoy my life and make the best of it I could. I was younger, of course, and stronger, and more fearless. I went back to school, joined Mensa, enjoyed my friends—and then came Wendell. I wonder if I can ever get to that place in myself again where I decide to accept myself and make my life as good as I can make it. I will need to find new ways. I do not want to go back for another degree. Local Mensa is ruined for me. There are AG's and RG's (*Mensa's national Annual Gatherings and Regional Gatherings*) but I don't know…it makes me feel very intimidated to think of being around a bunch of really bright people when I have lost my sharp edge. I wonder if I'll ever get that back to the full extent or if I will feel permanently diminished. Can I ever return to seeing the glass half full?

July 27

Tonight I spoke to J's *(a co-worker)* BSN *(Bachelor of Science in Nursing)* class about grief. It was hard to do, harder than I thought it would be. They asked some questions, like what helped me the most. I included this journal, even though I hadn't given it much thought before, but it does help.

I'm so relieved Mom is better. I can't believe how exhausted I got just being with her over the weekend. Of course, I hadn't had much rest the previous few days. I'm so glad she's OK for the time being. It would be very difficult to lose her at this time. The only good thing would be that the house and some funds would come to me and might tip the balance of security so I could get out at 55, but that's just a small thing compared to how difficult the rest would be. Besides missing her terribly, there would be all the rest to go through and I'd be ill before it was all over. In any case, she may go well another 5 or 10 years—who knows? As long as she can enjoy her life I hope she lives a long one. I can't stand the thought of her wasting away in a nursing home. I can't go there, so the future may be tough. For now, the crisis is over.

I'm looking forward to Florida next week.

Sun Aug 2

Starting month 8. I guess I will date things from Wendell's death. I used to use the divorce, then school, then our wedding day—from now on everything will be either before or after Wendell died.

K *(co-worker/potential boyfriend)* was supposed to come over Sat or call, but he didn't. In a way I'm relieved. I'd have been so nervous. I'm scared I'll get involved in something over my head, something not right for me, but because I'm so lonely I'm feeling vulnerable.

In three days I go to Florida. It will be a good break for me. I hope the house isn't too messy. I don't want to be uncomfortable and not be able to sleep while I'm there. I'm trying to pack sort of like I will do for the dive trip to see if I'll have enough room, etc. I could put my regulator in my tote bag and have a little more room I think, if I used the small reg bag and put it inside the tote like I did when we went to the Caribbean.

Still eating too much. Eat when I'm not hungry. That is very bad, very destructive. In a few weeks if this keeps up I won't have any clothes to wear. I don't clearly understand why I'm doing this. Am I putting up a shield to avoid having to deal with men? It worked for years after the divorce.

After I get back from the dive trip—what—deal with Patrick? He's doing some better—did some trimming today. I did all the mowing, pulled weeds, sprayed and used weed killer and clipped the bushes away from the walkway. I'll see how he does taking care of the place and animals while I'm gone. He may take Spooky *(the ceiling cat)* to the apt. Anything to get her out of the house and get my cats back to normal. I can't stand the cat boxes in the bathroom and cat food etc. all over the main floor.

A wave of missing Wendell is washing over me. God, it still hurts so much, I can barely stand it.

August 14

Almost 8 months.

Since Kim left I cry myself to sleep nearly every night. I miss her and I miss Wendell more. The visit to Florida was short and just underscored how much I miss her.

Next week I go to look at a house in Westernaire. I don't know if I'm ready to move. I have a gut feeling I can't handle this house another full year. They want a lot for the house, considering no basement. We'll see. I don't have to hurry. Patrick would be upset. Right now I don't care about that. He's still not carrying his weight in work or financially.

I have to do something about the cat. I don't think David is going to go down *(to Kim and Ron's)* any time soon. He talks and doesn't do.

I think I may be depressed again. I don't want medication. I'm trying to get through without. I'm back at Delta now—maybe I can lose a little wt—10 or 15 pounds would be enough—and stop gaining.

I have a hair appt. tomorrow. Wish I didn't. I hate going in there once a month, knowing they can tell the wt gain each time. I <u>hate</u> it. Nearly all my clothes are too tight. I resist buying new ones.

I wish I had something—someone—to live for, to look forward to.

Jury duty summons came. If I have to serve, the date is through 9/29—past the 25th when I'm supposed to leave for Nashville *(Nashville, IL, meeting a group going in vans to New Orleans to catch plane)* and Nassau. If I can't go I don't know what I'll do. I had forgot about it and then the summons came today.

K and I "chat" on email. It's a non-intimate, non-threatening way to get to know each other better. Eventually if we're going to do anything other than that, we'll have to go out. P says he's probably "intimidated" by me. Right now I feel like I couldn't intimidate a flea.

I take Buddy to the vet next week. I need to call the animal trainer again and get signed up.

I'm tired. No reason. Just tired.

Sat Aug 29

Past 8 months. I have decided to sell this house. I have also decided to buy a house in Marion. It's a nice house in a nice neighborhood, nothing unique about it.

I gave away Buddy. I couldn't handle him anymore. Tomorrow someone is coming to take J.C. *(male cat)*. He torments Frankie *(female Siamese cat)*, slaps water everywhere, and I need to reduce my cat population. If Patrick can find a place that takes cats, he'll take Dennis and Whitey. If not, I'll take Dennis to Florida if I can in Nov.

I called Vermont *(Vermont, IL where Wendell's parents lived)* today. Wendell's dad has cancer. I don't know what kind but the way his mother talked it has spread. I'm sorry for her since it looks as if she could lose both a son and a husband in one year—and she's always been the sickly one.

I have begun packing and sorting for another sale. I want to get new furniture, since the 2 couches and appliances are the only new furniture I've had in many years. I'll get a new kitchen table and chairs—round, I think. A new bedroom set, maybe stay with queen size and take my mattress and springs since they are new. All the appliances are staying at the *(new)* house except the washer and dryer, so I will take mine.

Monday Aug31

Went to the new house to meet building inspector. Owner wasn't there and wasn't expecting us. It was cluttered, messy, looked like just another house. I saw no sign she has begun to pack. Perhaps she's having movers do it. Anyway, her daughter came home and called her and she was really mad. I felt bad for her. I would have been upset too. I was able to note a few things—there are 3 chairs and a couch in the family room. There is a large dresser in the big bedroom and plenty of room for a large chest of drawers—I think there was one. There is also a couch and a computer console. I can put the small bed where the couch is and put one of the blue recliners and a lamp and end table in the corner.

I can take one of the blue recliners for the family room and take the other blue chair from the living room. If the blue couch in the apartment isn't messed up, I'll take it.

When I came home tonight I got choked up before I pulled into the drive. It was twilight and the house and the pond were so beautiful. But then I came inside and reality set in. The floor needed mopped and the carpet needed vac'd— and there's no space for anything in the kitchen. Tomorrow after J *(auctioneer)* leaves I need to work on de-cluttering the kitchen some more. That will put off a potential buyer faster than anything else. I can take one straight chair out and put away some other things out of sight. I need to put away most of the hats and keys and take some more stuff off the bulletin board.

I'm not sure if there is any white paint downstairs left from the basement painting, but there are a few places that need just a tiny touch up. I will put away all the tray tables in a closet and put away the bird stuff in the drawers, etc. I hate to think of the house being shown—there is so much I don't have time to do.

All this writing and I haven't mentioned Wendell. Talking with B I felt a great sadness when she talked of her husband and their relationship. It made me miss him so much. At least he's spared the pain of losing his dad which will probably be in a few months the way his mom talked. They never get medical stuff straight but he has cancer that has spread—and it sounds bad.

Tomorrow night is the widow support group in Herrin. I won't be able to go since J is coming around 6. I'm not sure that group is much help to me. All the women I've met so far are so much older than I am. I do better one on one talking with M or K or J. I called J tonight but she wasn't home.

Aug 31

Dear Wendell,

It's hard for me to tell you this but I think I'll feel better if I do. I have decided to sell the house. I know it's only been 8 months, but I've had a winter and a summer, and I don't think I can do it anymore. It's so beautiful and I can't keep it beautiful. It needs so much upkeep, and I can't afford the care it needs. The stairs are OK for now but my knee is giving me problems off and on, and if I had to have surgery, I wouldn't be able to make it up or down stairs. As I mow I think of you—all the time. How hard we worked on the yard, the lawn, the flowers. How much time and money we poured into our "yellow house"—and how we both loved it. I can hear you say, "Purty, idn'it?" in your funny way. You were so proud to have this beautiful place. I think you knew I wouldn't be able to stay here. I know I told you I couldn't bear to scatter your ashes over the pond. I'm so glad I didn't do that now. Soon your dad will rest near you and it will be easier for your mom to take care of both of you. I have tried the best I could to hang on, but the mowing makes me hurt for days afterward. I'm scratched and bug-bit and fighting poison ivy and wasps and snakes—and I just can't keep it up. When I pull out of the driveway for the last time I know it will be painful, and I will probably cry, as much for you as for the house. In a way it will always be "our yellow house", but I have to move, and move on with my life. I wish it didn't have to be. I wish you were here still to share it with me. But you're not and it's gone from being my joy and haven to a burden. I know you wouldn't want me to continue to bear this burden when I don't have to and so I'm selling and buying a place in town. I will have neighbors and a lawn I can manage, and a nice yard with a pool. It will be my house, and I will fix it to suit me. It's another way of moving on, which I must do.

Forgive me for not being stronger, strong enough to manage the place and hold onto it longer. I have to let go now, before I get sick or hurt. Please understand—I have to feel you would, since I know you loved me and would never want me to be hurt. I will miss the house, not because of what it is, but because of what it was for us—"our yellow house."

Sept 4

Well it has finally happened. K has asked me out. It's just a lunch date but it's a date. I'm excited and terrified. He's very nice and seems bright and funny—but he's 10 yrs younger and makes probably less than ½ what I do. Those things don't matter to me, at least I don't think they do. But I'm afraid they might matter to him. He's a nice looking guy, and I guess I'm thinking what does he see in me? Maybe I'm jumping the gun. It's just lunch, for heaven's sake. If it becomes more then I can worry. My chief concern now is not to get carried away. I feel so vulnerable. I'm worried I will lose my head and do something stupid. Another time in my life—more than once actually—I did stupid things in order to feel loved. Perhaps I'm smarter and stronger now. I hope to God so.

G called today. She's the lady I'm buying the house from. She seems nice but anxious and confused and stressed out over her divorce. She's going to be out by the 1st though so I can arrange the movers for the Mon and Tues.

Sun Sept 5

Tomorrow is my date with K. I'm still scared. I yearn so for someone to be close to that I could make a terrible mistake. Since he works at VA, everyone would know if we start "seeing" each other. I'm not used to my personal business being everyone's food for gossip. If we sleep together everyone will know. I know I'm getting ahead of myself but that's why I'm scared. I already have a mental image of certain things happening. I don't know him well. But if he's tender and kind, I will be lost. Then if it doesn't work out, I would be so embarrassed. People who think of me in one way would see me in a different way.

It's been over 9 months since I've had sex. When I was single before, I don't know if I had that long a time—I don't remember. But it's very hard. I miss the holding and cuddling and closeness as much as the actual sex—although I miss that, too. Since I lost all the weight I was beginning to enjoy it more than ever. I've gained some of it back but I still think I could feel "sexy" under the right circumstances. The trouble is knowing when the right circumstances are really right—for me in the long run, not just short-term gratification.

Sept 14

Well K broke the first date because he was sick—but he asked me again, and yesterday we went on a picnic to Giant City *(State Park.)* The night before I cried and cried and was nearly sick with anxiety. But the day went well, perhaps too well. I felt very comfortable with him and I had a really good time. I'd like to spend more time with him. I can feel my vulnerability, my need to be held and touched and loved. I know I need to be careful—very careful. But if I think if he remains interested I could have a serious dilemma on my hands. In a couple of weeks I'll be gone for a week and I can get a little distance if I need to. I can feel myself wanting to push too hard. I need to go slowly.

I'm trying to pack a little each night. Tomorrow I should probably mow if I get home early. I have to go for jury duty tomorrow. I hope I can get done with it before the 25th without any fuss. They can't stop me from leaving for Vienna/Nashville on time, but it could really mess up my schedule. There is still so much to pack. The office alone is a mess.

Oct 12

Nearly a month has passed. So much as happened.

I have bought the new house and moved. After a very shaky first night or two I'm doing fine now—it feels like home—my house. I'm almost done putting things away. I have a lot of boxes to get rid of and I'm sure I'll move things around until I get it all settled but I'm "nesting" well. It will be nice to get the carpets cleaned, the chimney cleaned, the furnace checked, etc. All that in the next 2 weeks. Some yard work to do, too, and a little painting. The big stuff is done. Auction on Oct 24, providing J is doing OK from his heart surgery. There is a buyer for the house. I signed a contract today, contingent on the sale of their old house. The realtors seem to feel the other house will sell quickly, so in a month or so I may be out from under house payments.

The Bahamas were beautiful and I enjoyed the trip in spite of Ron's selfishness in making me share my cabin with a strange man. I may never feel quite the same toward Ron ever again. *(The woman who was to be my cabin mate cancelled and the space was sold to a man. When they told me, I said, "Well, I'll just bunk with Kim." Our embarrassed group leader said that wouldn't be possible because Ron wouldn't allow it. Ron said he paid to take this vacation with his wife and that's what he was going to do. Poor Kim was in tears, feeling caught in the middle. One of the single guys in our group offered to share with me so at least I wasn't sharing with a total stranger. There were curtains around the bunks and we hardly saw each other, so it was less traumatic than it could have been. But*

I was very upset with Ron for a long time after. I eventually got over it.)

I'm excited about going to Australia in June. D may go but even if she doesn't, I'll have a great time. I hope my knees and hips will hold up. I'm especially having trouble with my right hip. Dr. H says it's bursitis, but it sure hurts-it's scary. I wish I could get off the 30 pounds I put back on. Maybe after I'm settled I can get back to Delta at least 2 days a week.

I called Wendell's folks Sun. They are the same. His dad is fair—still taking chemo and being stoic about it. They haven't said but I'm certain it's palliative. So sad for Rose, who doesn't cope well under good circumstances. When he dies, she won't be far behind, I predict. *(I was right. She died the following year.)*

Life without Wendell. Finally there is a life for me without Wendell. Out of the C'ville house I am not reminded of him—his empty chair, the empty side of the bed, all the extra work, constantly wishing he were there to help me. All this is new now—new problems, true, but all the time moving in etc. I didn't consider if Wendell were here he could fix this or handle that and so on. I just tackled each thing as it came along and dealt with it. I'm glad to be out of the C'ville house before Christmas. I think it would have been terribly hard there. Kim and Ron will be here and I'd like to be in a decent frame of mind for their visit—not all mopey and blue. I'm sure I'll have some distress—that's to be expected. I'm probably feeling a little euphoria now from the move, the pending sale, etc. Right now my pain from missing him is at a low ebb, but it will return, I'm certain of that.

Mon Oct 19

Tomorrow the chimney sweep comes and then except for B *(a handyman)* doing some yard chores, fixing screens, etc. all the work of making the house ready to live in is done. I still have some pictures to hang, and later B and J *(his wife)* will paint inside the hall, the other two bedrooms, and some of the woodwork. For the most part, though, it's done. Everyone who sees the house loves it—and I'm coming to love it too. I don't even mind the trains so much. They are mostly short ones. *(Tracks ran about 50 yards behind the house.)*

I played the piano a while tonight and got a little weepy. It's odd how I feel about Wendell at this point. I'm very comfortable in this new house, more so than I was in Carterville and way more than in Harrisburg. I look at pictures of Wendell and I'm not sure I'm as sad as I once was. To be sure I'm still lonely and I miss the physical and emotional closeness of being with another person. But there were things I don't miss—there are things I have now that I would never have had if he had lived. In some way I feel terrible in writing this, but it's true and to deal with the guilt I need to face it. I'm certainly not "glad" he's gone, but I have adjusted, and I'm beginning to like my life. That's not a bad thing.

I'd like to think about having a get together here. I would invite *(Here I listed a bunch of friend's names. The party never materialized.)* Out of 30 or so about 18 or 20 would probably make it. It could be a potluck with me furnishing coffee, beer, and soda. Perhaps the second weekend in Nov—I'll think about it.

Thurs. Oct 29

Here I am in my house. I mowed the front lawn for the first time today. It took about 40 minutes. The mower is running ragged. Patrick borrowed it. This Sat will be the last time I will allow that.

Nearly all the inside stuff is done except replacing some blinds and painting. I hope B and J can get the painting done before Christmas. I guess I will ask them to feed the animals while I go to Florida in Nov.—that's only 3 weeks away.

I will net over $12,000 from the auction—should have the check by next week. After I pay the remaining installment on the Australia trip, I will have over $8 thousand to put in the money market. That will bring it close to back to $20 thousand. When I sell the house, I will have a sizeable chunk left over after paying off this mortgage—about $55 thousand. I'm nervous about putting it into the market. I need to ask B about bonds—and put some more back into the money market. It really hurts to see the portfolio shrink like it has—lost $20 thousand in past 4 months—but what was I supposed to do? Put it under my mattress?

Party at V and L 's Sat night. That's Halloween and I had sort of looked forward to the trick or treaters. I think tomorrow I'll take some candy next door to the kids and explain that I won't be home and may miss them Sat but I want them to have a "treat". The little boy is often out in the yard but he won't answer me when I say "Hi!" I don't know if he's shy or what. I need to learn their names.

Haven't met my other next-door neighbor either. I'm told she's a nurse. She leaves before 7 every morning. There seems to be a teenaged boy and a girl there, too, but I'm not sure. G *(across the street)* is very friendly. She brought over Italian beef last night. It was OK—not as good as what I make—but it was a nice thought.

I had a big cry this week.. Missed Wendell so much.

Very shaky at work this week. A confrontation with a doc and SW—no really big deal, but for a while it made me feel ill. I was never much good at that and now I'm worse. Nearly folded up Weds.

My eating is bothering me. I managed to pass up ice cream at Kroger's but later bought some chocolate things at Wal-Mart. Sometimes I care a lot and other times I don't care at all. I keep remembering how much people commented when I lost all the weight, telling me how good I looked, etc. I keep thinking, now I'm starting to look like I did before— what they must be thinking and saying. If I keep on, I won't be physically able to dive and I don't want to lose that. I'm not sure what to do. I always thought that if I could eat all by myself—not have to put up with Wendell's sweets, etc. and hot dogs, and eating out, that I could eat "normally".

Nov. 7

Into the 11th month. I am daily more comfortable in my house. I especially like the fireplace. In the spring it will be the pool, but for now the fireplace is great . I have not been spending the hours on the computer game that I had been. I get bills paid, laundry done, other paperwork done, plans made, etc. I fix a decent meal most nights—tonight it was beef kabobs and hash browns.

The auction went well—and I have already noted that I don't have the check yet, but should next week.

I hope the house sells soon. I'm not happy paying 2 light and water bills and a house payment.

The stock market is looking up and that is very good. I was getting rather nervous watching my money dwindle away. I may have already recouped my losses. I'll get a statement soon from the TSP *(Thrift Savings Plan, a government IRA)* but it may not reflect the recent gain so I must not let that concern me.

Sunday I'm supposed to see K for a movie and dinner here— if he calls to tell what time, which movie. It's something to do, but nothing serious will come of it—he has already told me he's drinking a lot again, and I can't handle that on any kind of serious basis. *(Jack's alcoholism was what ruined our marriage.)*

William *(Jack's little brother)* is moving back to Christopher. He calls about once a week and sometimes we talk a long time. He's lonely since his wife and he split up. It's rather odd feeling half like a big sister and half like a friend. He likes to discuss his problems with women. I'm certainly no expert and the conversation occasionally gets "plain" to use Jack's grandmother's term. I'm not at all sure how I feel about that. I did tell him to call after he gets settled and I'd have him over for supper. If he were a few years older, I wouldn't feel so strange about it. He's 43. K mentioned he just turned 42. I guess I missed his birthday—I was busy unpacking, etc. And anyway I was ticked off at him for saying he'd call and not doing it <u>twice</u>. It wouldn't surprise me in the least if he didn't call about Sunday either. I'll get the stuff for supper and call Mom to tell her I won't be at her house Sun evening.

I forgot to call Vermont last Sunday. Mom was here and I just totally forgot to call. Even though I'd just as soon not call, I'd better do it tomorrow or Sunday. Wendell wasn't even close to them—how can I feel close? They mean practically nothing to me, as harsh as that sounds. I wish them well, of course, but I have to get on with my life and when I call it's so hard—and often painful. I know the holidays coming up will be especially hard for his mother, but I can't go up there—I just can't.

I need to get out my video camera and charge the batteries and video the house.

I also need to get down to Mermet, *(Mermet Springs, the quarry where we learned to dive)* pick up my tank and some bulbs for my light and the sheet for Kim and take Glen his hat. I'd want to take the light to Cozumel.

I haven't talked to Kim in nearly 2 weeks since right after the auction. She left me a message on email—her resume. I guess she's job hunting again. Ron pushes her to get work different from what she's doing because she doesn't make much. *(She was working as a vet tech.)* Maybe he's right. If he ever leaves her, or dies, she'll be in a pickle to make a living.

I had coffee late in the afternoon and I'm paying for it now—it's 1 am and I'm not sleepy. I need to read—that always makes me drowsy.

Nov 22

Tomorrow—in fact in about 2 hours—it will be 11 months since Wendell died. Counting down now to 1 yr. At times I thought I would go crazy, never made it. Sometimes I still feel that way. It's for sure I'm not as "well adjusted" right now as I was 2 or 3 months ago. Perhaps it's the effect of all the change—moving, etc.

I go to see Dr. H tomorrow and, hopefully, get a repeat mammogram and ultrasound. They found something—again—and it will probably mean another biopsy. Every time I have one the odds of the next one being positive go up. I guess if it happens, it just happens. I'll deal with it the best way I can.

This week I had a "flashback" when I saw a Salvation Army bell ringer and heard Christmas carols in the Sam's Store parking lot. It was awful. I was "back" in St. Louis, hearing all the background noise for my descent into pain and despair as every day the news got worse and the "merrier" all those around me were, the grimmer and more detached I felt. The episode in the parking lot only lasted a moment, but it made me feel sick. All week I've cried off and on, several times really hard as if it was the first month all over again. When I'm not crying, I'm eating. I'm blowing up like a beachball. I hate it, hate it, hate it. I'm going to ask K *(nurse practitioner)* to give me something to get through this month. In 2 days Mom and I and I are going to Kim's. I want to see her. I really don't want to see him. I'm still so hurt and angry at him—and he will never understand, never apologize—and even if he did, it's done. He can't take it back even if he wanted to. What a terrible position he put both me and Kim in. How mean and petty and inconsiderate—and how it upset me. I'm not looking forward to this trip. Mom can't carry or pull anything anymore and I'll have all the luggage to have to carry and I have to worry about her. I should smack myself for thinking that. I'm lucky she's still with me and in relatively good health.

Dec. 1 Tues

I'm afraid I'm feeling sorry for myself—fat, lonely, grieving and sorry for myself. I hurt—my knees hurt, my head hurts and especially my back hurts. I have to wait a week to find out about the test. Maybe there is something wrong. I don't feel right inside-I can't tell any more if it's real or not. I had a miserable day taking Tylenol and eating Maalox. I thought about cancelling my dry suit class but I'm afraid if I do I won't go diving as much and I'll lose what I have, gain more weight and not be able to wear anything. I ought to go buy some more clothes, but I'm too proud and too tired—so tired. I should just go to bed after I eat instead of watching some stupid TV show.

Patrick is coming tomorrow to help me get a tree. I'd as soon skip it but I feel like I must—I can't keep sliding into this depression I feel hanging over me. I could just let go so easily. I'm not sure it's worth the effort anymore.

Dec 8

The days walk past me.

I bow and bend and sink,

The sun hides, bruised clouds matt my windows

Rain spits and wind whines, trains shudder through my nights.

I am filled with emptiness.

The new days yawn before me.

They seem to think I ought to care.

The calendar a metronome,

Days marching by to the inexorable end.

Trains trumpeting their passing.

Warning me of crossings before dawn.

I used to hate the sound that went with engines.

Now they pierce me.

Tues Dec 15

I've been sick for 3 days. I'm not sure if it's coincidence that Dec 12 was the day Wendell was first hospitalized but I still feel really crappy—hot one minute, cold the next, headache, tired, a little dizzy, nausea off and on—and I've been bleeding for 5 days when I'm not supposed to. I don't know if I'm sick or crazy. I have to go to work tomorrow—or go to a doctor. I wanted to get groceries this evening but I honestly feel too weak. I have to go after work tomorrow and then rush home to go to dinner at 5:30. I don't want to cancel that if I can help it since I won't see B, D, and M before Christmas if I don't go. I hope I get to feeling a lot better before the kids get here—that's in 9 days. In 8 days it will be one year. A year is an arbitrary measure. Dec 23 is just another day, I keep telling myself. Don't be so melodramatic about it. It's a year, get over it, get on with it. I really hate feeling all maudlin and weepy. And then, I think about him, about his skin, his face, his shoulders, his legs—I can see him so plainly and I miss him so much. Where am I going to put all this pain? If I put it inside, it makes me sick. I feel like I'm going nuts.

December 21 Monday

Home again today—still sick. Just when I think I'm OK and my mind is playing tricks on me I have a wave of nausea or a pulse of headache and I realize I really <u>am </u>sick. Went to Dr. again—got stronger antibiotics and decongestant.

Tomorrow is the 22nd. That begins the night of the end. I imagine I will not be able to sleep until after 1 am on the 23rd. Why is "a year" such a milestone? Will I miss him less on the24th, or in January or March or next Christmas? The tears come. I don't want them to but they come anyway. I'm so tired of wearing this badge of widowhood. I hate it, hate it, hate it. I hate what my life has become. I feel like a second-class person, like half a person. Have I come very far in a year? It seems not.

December 24, 1998

The night of the 22nd was bad but not as bad as I had anticipated. The candle ritual helped. I lit 3—one for Wendell, one for me—one for us. I blew them out one at a time after telling him I love and miss him, that I was OK, and that I had to get on with my life. It left me with a feeling of peace that I didn't think I'd be able to achieve and I was able to sleep. Today I feel physically much better, a little shaky, but definitely better. Mom is here and the kids are on their way. It will be a real Christmas, albeit with an overtone of sadness but joy that those of us who are here can be together. Patrick misses the rest of his family, I know, but we'll be here for him as he will for us. Perhaps we'll call Texas tonight or definitely tomorrow. I probably should call Wendell's folks too, but that will be hard. I don't want to lose the sense of peace I have about Wendell. Completing the year has somehow lifted part of the burden. I sorrowed the first year—I can survive those that remain. Thank goodness Mom is in good health and has been here for me. It would have been unthinkable to lose her this year.

The year is drawing to a close in more ways than one. My future is whatever I will make it to be. In so many ways I'm fortunate—financially secure, basically healthy, good job, lots of friends, and my family, small as it is, around me. I cannot change what happened. I can't bring him back to me. But I can move toward to the rest of my life. That's what he would tell me to do and what he would want.

EPILOGUE

My journey through grief didn't end at the end of the first year. By then, however, I knew I was going to be all right. Not only would I survive, I looked forward to experiencing happiness and joy again.

Kim and Ron remain in Florida, living in the house they bought when they first arrived. Ron has done well and receives continued promotions and bonuses in his company. For several years Kim has taught Health Education at Northwest Florida State College part time , making good use of her own MS Ed in Health Education. Childless by choice, they enjoy their lives together. I long ago forgave Ron what I had perceived through the lens of my grief as selfishness. He's kind and good to me. I love him as if he were my son.

I did retire at 55, not because I no longer wanted to work, but because I was no longer physically able. Due to major back surgery, I had the option to retire on disability, which I did. A second back surgery a few years later resulted in improved mobility; however, I didn't return to work.

After many dedicated years, Mom gave up her hospital volunteer work and moved into an assisted living center. She kept her mind active following her beloved St. Louis Baseball Cardinals on TV and watching NASCAR. (She had an enormous crush on Jeff Gordon.) A series of small strokes did eventually confine her to a nursing home, where she died peacefully in her sleep in late February, 2012, a week from her 98th birthday.

I promised Patrick's mother before she died I would take care of him. I believe I was able to do that. He finished his master's degree in communication at Southern Illinois University and ultimately found his niche working in various positions for the university. A confirmed bachelor and outdoorsman, he holds a special place in my heart.

For a number of years I volunteered with Southern Illinois Hospice as a patient visitor and a community speaker. I also helped establish a hospice ward at the Marion, Illinois Department of Veterans Affairs Medical Center.

Eventually after I retired I was able to travel extensively, initially with a local group of friends, and later on my own. I saw much of our amazing planet, including one place most people don't get to see firsthand—Antarctica. That was by far my favorite journey. Perhaps I'll write about that trip. Wendell would have loved reading about it.

After Mom died I moved to Florida later that year to be closer to Kim and Ron. After several years, maintaining my house there became too difficult. I currently live in a comfortable apartment in a senior living apartment complex in Crestview, FL, near Kim and Ron. I have been coping with some health problems, but basically, life is good.

Let me say that much of what I write about "widows" also pertains to "widowers", same sex widows or widowers, and those who have lost a significant other, regardless of whether or not they were married.

Each person's experience with loss and grief is unique to her or him. Nevertheless, there are common threads woven into grief, regardless of the circumstances. Acute emotional pain (sometimes experienced as actual physical pain), confusion, difficulty concentrating and making decisions, fear that one is becoming mentally unbalanced, and fear of the future all are commonly experienced by those in the throes of grief. Other emotions and events commonly experienced during acute grief include vivid dreams and/or nightmares; feeling abandoned by and angry at the lost loved one; hallucinations, particularly seeing and even speaking with the lost loved one; and reluctance to leave the perceived safety of home. It's also common, especially a few months following the loss, for others to hint and eventually practically insist the grieving individual needs to "get over it" and move on with life. These comments are rooted in the discomfort others feel in dealing with those who are grieving. Our society has coached us to believe that grieving "too long" is a bad thing. Six months after my husband died, I was in a deep depression, and my own mother told me I needed to "get over it" and get on with living. The reality is grief has no timetable. Grief is a complex combination of feelings and actions that should be considered acceptable as long as the grieving individual needs it to be.

I was extremely fortunate when my husband died that he left a large amount of life insurance that ensured my financial stability from the very beginning of my widowhood. Also, I had no young children at home to deal with and I was in reasonably good health myself at the time of his death. I'm acutely aware that not every widow, not every person who experiences the loss of a significant other, is as fortunate as I was regarding those issues. Those left in destitute situations, perhaps with crushing debt, will certainly have a grief experience different from mine in many ways. Widows who have never worked outside their homes may be faced with the daunting challenge of entering the world of work, possibly with limited skills and opportunities. Those with young children at home face an entirely different set of challenges. Widows whose husbands had total control over family and household expenses and never shared important information such as bank account balances, mortgage and charge card debt, and other relevant and critical information face a special set of challenges in addition to dealing with their grief.

I don't claim to be able to assist everyone experiencing grief to suddenly feel better after reading my book. It's not a "how to" book, but it is a book to be read and re-read, for notes to be written in the margins and for passages to be underlined.

Thank you for sharing my journey.

Vennie Anderson, June, 2021

RECOMMENDATIONS FOR FURTHER ASSISTANCE IN DEALING WITH GRIEF

Books:

A Grief Observed by C. S. Lewis, 1963.

When Bad Things Happen to Good People by Harold S. Kushner, 1984

It's OK That You're Not OK by Megan Devine, 2017

Grieving Us: A Field Guide for Living With Loss Without Losing Yourself by Kimberly Pittman-Schulz, 2021

All the above are available in various formats in bookstores, libraries and on amazon.com. Used and less expensive copies may also be available on eBay and in used bookstores.

An online resource that was extremely helpful for me at the time was widownet.net, now widownet.org. However, when I attempted to look at the site for possible inclusion in this list, I found it has not been well maintained. Because of that, coupled with a confusing, not-user-friendly interface, I can't recommend it at this time.

Perhaps the best recommendation I can make is to begin a journal yourself. A bound blank journaling book is a lovely tool, but you can simply use an ordinary spiral or loose-leaf notebook. A journal doesn't need to be fancy to be helpful. You don't need to be a gifted writer like C.S Lewis in order to put your thoughts and feelings down on paper. Just begin writing what you feel. You may find a helpful source of comfort within yourself.

Ingram Content Group UK Ltd.
Milton Keynes UK
UKHW020939200423
420437UK00001B/15